Hanukkah Crafts

Hanukkah Crafts

★ A Holiday Craft Book ★

★ Judith Hoffman Corwin ★

FRANKLIN WATTS

A Division of Grolier Publishing

New York ★ London ★ Hong Kong ★ Sydney

Danbury, Connecticut

★**Also by Judith Hoffman Corwin**★

African Crafts
Asian Crafts
Latin American and Caribbean Crafts

Colonial American Crafts: The Home
Colonial American Crafts: The School
Colonial American Crafts: The Village

Papercrafts

Christmas Crafts
Easter Crafts
Halloween Crafts
Kwanzaa Crafts
Thanksgiving Crafts
Valentine Crafts

★ **For Jules Arthur and Oliver Jamie** ★

Library of Congress Cataloging-in-Publication Data

Corwin, Judith Hoffman.
    Hanukkah crafts/Judith Hoffman Corwin.
       p.   cm.—(A holiday craft book)
    Includes index.
    Summary: Explains the history and customs connected with Hanukkah and pro-
    vides ideas and instructions for making greeting cards, gift wrappings, presents,
    decorations, and holiday treats.
    ISBN 0-531-11269-1 (lib. ed.).—ISBN 0-531-15757-1 (pbk.)
    1. Hanukkah–Juvenile literature. 2. Jewish crafts–Juvenile literature. [1. Hanukkah.
2. Jewish crafts.} I. Title. II. Series: Corwin, Judith Hoffman. Holiday crafts.
BM695.H3C67 1996
296.4'35—dc20   95-38077
                                                     CIP
Copyright © 1996 by Judith Hoffman Corwin   AC
All rights reserved
Printed in the United States of America
6 5 4 3 2 1

Contents

About Hanukkah

Hanukkah is an ancient holiday, one of the most happy and festive in the Jewish calendar. It is called the "Festival of Lights" because candles are lit, at sundown, on the eight nights of the holiday. Hanukkah falls in the middle of winter, usually in December (Kislev on the Jewish calendar). Into this harsh month Hanukkah brings light, warmth, and happiness. Candlelight glows in the house and there is a holiday spirit, with special foods, songs, and gift giving.

There is no one right way to spell Hanukkah in English. That's because it is a Hebrew word. Since the Hebrew alphabet is very different from the alphabet used to write English words, we try to copy the sound of the Hebrew word using our alphabet.

The Hanukkah story is one of great strength and courage. Over two thousand years ago, the Temple in Jerusalem was taken away from the Jews. The conquerors filled the Temple with statues of their own gods and tried to force the Jews to worship them. The Jews refused and were treated harshly. A small group, led by Judah Maccabee, decided to fight for their freedom. Maccabee means "hammer" in Hebrew, and for three years the soldiers, called the Maccabees, hammered at the enemy until, at last, Jerusalem was free.

When the Maccabees reentered the Temple, they found that the lamp of Eternal Light was not burning. They searched for the jars of special oil to fill the lamp, but found only one jar—enough for a single day. Miraculously, the jar of oil lasted for eight days, during which time the Jews celebrated the rededication of the Temple. The word Hanukkah means "dedication." Since that time, the eight-day holiday starting with the twenty-fifth day of Kislev is a joyous festival in memory of this Hanukkah miracle.

Today Hanukkah is celebrated by lighting the menorah, a Hanukkah lamp, or candleholder, with places for nine candles. Eight stand for the days the miraculous oil burned. The ninth candle, or shammash, is used to light the others. The first night the shammash and one candle are lit. Every night after that, another candle is added until on the eighth day all the candles are lit.

Hanukkah is a family holiday and is celebrated with great anticipation and excitement. Young people decorate their homes with colorful

paper menorahs pasted on doors and windows. A menorah and a box of colored candles wait ready for the first night of Hanukkah.

There is no special feast for Hanukkah. A favorite treat to serve at this time is the latke, or potato pancake. In some places it is the custom to prepare a meal of dairy foods in which different cheeses are served. There is much merrymaking and exchanging of gifts. A favorite Hanukkah game is the spinning of the dreidel—a top with four sides.

You may like to help friends learn about the holiday. You can invite them to the lighting of the menorah. Tell the story behind the holiday and let them share the special things that make it a happy time— playing dreidel, eating some of the foods, and singing a song. This is a time to create your own family traditions and to share with others.★

Oh, drei-del drei-del drei-del, I made it out of clay.

And when my drei-del's rea-dy, Oh, drei-del I will play.

Let's Get Started

This book tells you about the Hanukkah holiday, its legends, and its history. It is full of ideas for making greeting cards, decorations, gift wrappings, presents, and wonderful treats to eat. Often, you will be able to make everything yourself, using everyday household supplies and objects. Use your imagination and you will be surprised at what you can create. The treasures you make will add color and excitement to your holiday celebration.

Directions for some of the projects include patterns for you to use to make a copy of what is shown. You don't want to cut up this book, so copy the pattern with tracing paper. Begin by placing a piece of tracing paper over the pattern in the book. Using a pencil with a soft lead, trace the outline of the pattern. Turn the paper over and rub all over the pattern with the pencil. Turn it over again, and tape or hold it down carefully on the paper or fabric you have chosen to work with. Draw over your original lines, pressing hard on the pencil. Lift the tracing-paper pattern and you are ready to go on with the other instructions for your project.★

The Hanukkah Menorah

Through the centuries Hanukkah menorahs have been made in many styles, shapes, and materials, using silver, gold, clay, brass, tin, wood, lead, and other materials. Some have been elaborate, while others have been very simple, with plain holders for the candles or for oil. They have been decorated with sayings in Hebrew, the Star of David, or even a likeness of Judah Maccabee. Elephants appear on some, representing the warrior elephants used to storm the Temple.

The menorah can be any size or shape. The candles can stand in a straight line, or in a curve, or even a circle. Most Hanukkah candles are small (about 3¼″ long) and are usually sold in boxes holding 44 candles of different colors. It is important that the candles are separated in the menorah, so that their flames don't merge into a larger flame. This separateness honors each night. The traditional Hanukkah menorah holds the candles at the same height, with only the shammash higher. That shows that all the nights of Hanukkah are equally important.★

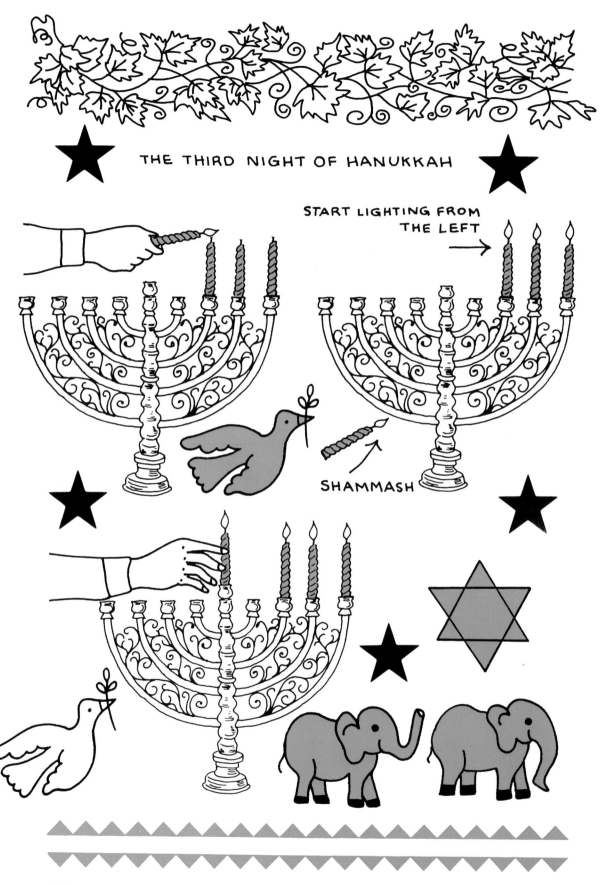

THE THIRD NIGHT OF HANUKKAH

START LIGHTING FROM THE LEFT

SHAMMASH

14

Lighting the Hanukkah Candles

On each of the eight nights of Hanukkah, candles are lit. The candles are placed in a special menorah that is used only for Hanukkah. There is one holder for each of the eight nights and one for the shammash. Shammash means servant in Hebrew, and this candle is used to light the others. Its holder should be different in some way from the others, either higher or lower.

The candles to be lit on a night are placed in the menorah beginning at the right, and moving to the left. On the first night start with one candle, plus the shammash, and add one more each day. New candles are used each night and the candles are allowed to burn down. The shammash is lighted first, and used to light the other candles, moving from left to right. That means that the newest candle is lit first each night. Then the shammash is returned to its special holder.

Prayers are said as the shammash is lighted. They can be said in Hebrew or English, or in both languages. These are the two blessings that are said each night:

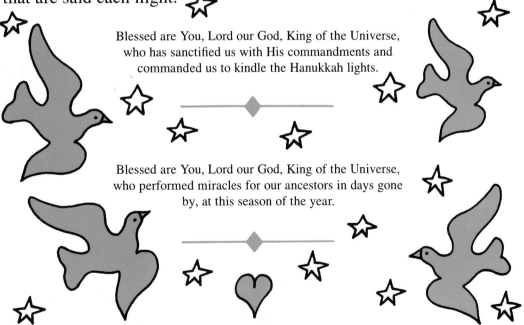

Blessed are You, Lord our God, King of the Universe, who has sanctified us with His commandments and commanded us to kindle the Hanukkah lights.

Blessed are You, Lord our God, King of the Universe, who performed miracles for our ancestors in days gone by, at this season of the year.

The candle-lighting ceremony takes place at sundown each night of Hanukkah. Forty-four candles are needed for the holiday. Families share the lighting so that everyone gets a chance. Some take turns on different nights. Other families pass the shammash around so several members get a chance on one night. ★

A Clay Menorah to Make

We will make a simple clay menorah out of ingredients from the kitchen. You will need a box of Hanukkah candles.

INGREDIENTS★

1 cup all-purpose flour
½ cup salt
¼ cup water
1 tablespoon vegetable oil

UTENSILS★

large mixing bowl
mixing spoon, measuring cups and spoons
aluminum foil, shoe-box cover, sand and pebbles
pot holders
gold or silver paint markers

HERE'S HOW TO DO IT★

1. Put all the ingredients into the mixing bowl. Stir until everything is combined. Now your clay is ready to work with.

2. Pull off a piece of clay and roll it to make a ball. Make ten clay balls, each about the size of a walnut. Put one aside. Place your thumb in the center of a ball and press to make a small hollow, the size to hold one candle. Place a candle inside to be sure it fits. Remove the candle. Repeat with each of the other balls. Now you have nine candleholder pots.

3. Place one pot on top of the reserved clay ball and gently press it down to attach it. This will be the tall holder for the shammash.

4. To make a base for the candleholders, shape the rest of your clay into a roll about 12″ long and 3″ thick. Gently flatten this, and make a boatlike shape. The outside edges should go up slightly, as in the illustration. The finished base should be about 2″ wide by 12″ long and about ¼″ thick.

17

5. Place the shammash in the center of the base, gently pressing it on. Place the rest of the little pots on the base, as shown, four on each side of the shammash. Leave the completed menorah to dry for a few days, or bake it on aluminum foil in the oven, at 350°F for about 10 minutes. **Ask an adult to help you use the oven.**

6. You can leave your candleholder plain—it will look like a menorah of ancient times. Or, you can let it cool and then paint it with a gold or silver paint marker.

7. To make a different menorah, make all of the clay candleholders, including the shammash. Wrap a shoe-box cover with aluminum foil, to make it look pretty. Place a layer of sand in the cover and arrange the clay candleholders on top. You can add some small pebbles to make it look more interesting. Check the illustration for some ideas. ★

Hanukkah Bear Candleholder

This little bear will be fun to use during your Hanukkah celebration. The pocket holds the candles for each night's candle lighting. Make an extra bear and give it as a special gift.

HERE'S WHAT YOU WILL NEED★

1 square of tan felt
scrap of brown felt for the inside of the ears, paws, and pocket
scrap of black felt for the nose
scrap of red felt for the tongue
2 black buttons for the eyes
pencil, tracing paper, scissors, pins
needle, tan thread
stuffing material (polyester pillow stuffing, old panty hose, cotton balls, or tissues)
white glue

HERE'S HOW TO DO IT★

1. Follow the directions on page 11 and trace the pattern for the bear. Cut it out.

2. Fold the square of tan felt in half and pin the pattern onto it. Cut it out. You will have two bear shapes.

3. With one bear shape on top of the other, sew around all the outside edges. Leave open the space marked by the dots, so that you can stuff your bear.

4. If you don't want to sew the bear together you could run a thin line of glue along the outside edge of one bear shape, leaving the same opening for stuffing. Place the other bear shape on top and press them together. Allow the glue to set for half an hour before you continue.

5. Gently push the stuffing into the bear, filling the ears and head first. Now fill the front paws, stomach, and feet. Sew the opening closed, or use glue.

6. From the brown felt, cut out inside ear pieces, paws, and pocket. Run a thin line of glue along the two sides and bottom of the pocket piece and glue it onto the bear, as shown. Glue the inside ear pieces and paws in place, as shown.

7. From the black felt, cut out the nose, and glue it in place. Cut out the tongue from the red felt and glue it on. Glue on the black buttons for eyes. Fill the bear with two candles for the first night of Hanukkah and enjoy your new friend.★

Noah's Ark Hanukkah Card

Noah and his wife and their boatload of animals will make a lively Hanukkah card. In the Bible story of the flood, Noah brings two of each animal aboard the ark, so you will need to make two of each.

HERE'S WHAT YOU WILL NEED★

tracing paper, pencil
8½″ × 11″ sheet of white paper
fine-line black marker, colored pencils or markers
piece of ribbon or yarn

HERE'S HOW TO DO IT★

1. Follow the directions on page 11 to copy the designs. Transfer them onto the white paper.

2. Go over the lines with the black marker. Color in the designs with markers or colored pencils. Write a Hanukkah greeting on the bottom and sign the card.

3. Roll up the sheet of paper, tie a ribbon around it, and give it to a special friend.★

VAV HEH DALET GIMMEL BET ALEF

LAMED KAF YOOD TET CHET ZA-YIN

TZA-DEE PAY A-YIN SA-MECH NUN MEM

TAV SHIN RAY-SH KUF

A Look at the Hebrew Alphabet

Hebrew is the language of the Jewish people. It looks very different from English. Here are the twenty-two Hebrew letters, with their English names written underneath. Try writing them with a black fine-line felt-tip marker. Hebrew is written from right to left, unlike English, which is from left to right. Writing the letters in different colors will make a very pleasing design to use on a Hanukkah greeting card or on wrapping paper. We will also use four of the letters—Nun, Gimmel, Heh, and Shin—when we make dreidels. These same letters can also be used on Hanukkah cookies.★

NUN   GIMMEL   HEH   SHIN

Speedy Dreidel

It takes just a few minutes to make this dreidel. The dreidel is used to play a Hanukkah game called "spin the dreidel." It is spun like a top for prizes such as pennies, nuts, candies, hard candies, or chocolates. The goodies are put on the floor near where the game is to be played. The dreidel has four sides, each with a Hebrew letter on it. They are Nun, Gimmel, Heh, and Shin. These letters stand for the Hebrew words "Nes Gadol Hayah Sham," which means "A Very Great Miracle Happened There." These letters stand for other words when playing dreidel. The custom of spinning tops on Hanukkah originated in Germany.

HERE'S WHAT YOU WILL NEED★

3″ square of cardboard
ruler, scissors
colored markers, or pencils
a short stub of a pencil, about 3″ long

HERE'S HOW TO DO IT★

1. With a marker draw lines from corner to corner on the square of cardboard. This divides the square into four sections and also marks the center of it. Check the illustration.

2. Draw a Hebrew letter in each section as shown.

3. With the point of the scissors, carefully poke a hole through the center. Now insert the pencil, twisting it to work it down. The pencil should stick out the bottom as far as it needs to spin easily; usually a little more than an inch works. Try it out to see where it spins best. Be sure to round the point of the pencil a little.★

שׁ ה ג נ

How to Play a Dreidel Game

All the players should start out with the same number of objects. You will need only one dreidel since the players take turns spinning it. Make sure you all agree on the rules before the game begins.

HERE'S WHAT YOU WILL NEED★

dreidel
pile of objects—pennies, stones, bottle caps, nuts, or candies

HERE'S HOW TO DO IT★

1. Each player puts one item from his or her pile of objects into the center, called the pot.

2. A player spins the dreidel; the letter that faces up when the dreidel stops tells what to do:

Nun (none): The player takes nothing; the next player spins.

Gimmel (give): The player takes everything in the pot; all the players put in one more item before the next person spins.

Heh (half): The player takes half of what's in the pot (the larger half if there's an odd number in the pot).

Shin (add): The player puts one item into the pot.

3. If the pot is empty, or there's only one object in it, every player has to put one in before the next spin.

4. The game is over when one player has won everything, and everyone else is wiped out.★

Oh, Hanukkah

Oh, Ha-nuk-kah, Oh, Ha-nuk-kah, come light the me-no-rah!

Let's have a par-ty, we'll all dance the ho-rah. Gath-er

'round the ta-ble, we'll give you a treat, A drei-del to

play with, and lat-kes to eat. And while we are

play-ing The can-dles are burn-ing low. One for

each night, They shed a sweet light, To re-mind us

of days long a-go. One for each night, They shed

a sweet light, To re-mind us of days long a-go.

Hanukkah Songs

Here are two traditional Hanukkah songs. "Oh, Hanukkah" is usually sung after the Hanukkah candles have been lighted. "Oh, Dreidel" is sung while spinning the dreidel. Dreidels, like menorahs, can be made out of various materials. An ancient dreidel might have been made out of clay; certainly the word clay works for the rhyme in the verse. Each of the verses to the song are sung to the same tune. ★

Oh, Dreidel

Oh, drei-del drei-del drei-del, I made it out of clay.

And when my drei-del's rea-dy, Oh, drei-del I will play.

1   Oh, dreidel, dreidel, dreidel,
I made it out of clay.
And when it's dry and ready,
Oh, dreidel I will play!

2   I'll take my little dreidel
And give it a good strong spin.
I hope it lands on Gimmel,
For then I'm sure to win.

3   If I spin Heh, I take half,
But none if I spin Nun.
I get the pot with Gimmel
With Shin I must pay one.

Ancient City Hanukkah Invitation

You can use this beautiful drawing on invitations to your Hanukkah celebration, or on holiday cards to send to family and friends. If you trace it and copy it onto heavy paper, or watercolor paper, you can paint in the design and give it as a gift. Sign your name at the bottom.

HERE'S WHAT YOU WILL NEED★

paper and envelopes
tracing paper, pencil
black fine-line marker
watercolors, paintbrush, container of water, or colored pencils or
    markers

HERE'S HOW TO DO IT★

Follow the directions on page 10 and trace the illustration for the ancient city. Go over the pencil lines with the black marker. Color or paint as you like.★

Hanukkah Gelt

Hanukkah gelt (gelt means money) is given as a gift at the holiday celebration. Today coins made of chocolate are wrapped in gold foil for the occasion. Using the clay recipe on page 17, we can make our own Hanukkah gelt. The coins can be given as presents, put inside a Hanukkah card, used as prizes when playing dreidel, or as decorations for the Hanukkah table. Three designs are given—a modern shekel (a coin used today in Israel); a coin from ancient times with letters that say "Holy City" together with the earliest known drawing of a candlestick or menorah; and one with a picture of three pomegranates on it, also from ancient times.

HERE'S WHAT YOU WILL NEED★

batch of clay (page 17), rolling pin
pencil, knife, newspaper
gold and silver paint markers, black fine-line permanent marker

HERE'S HOW TO DO IT★

1. Follow the directions on page 17 and make the clay. On a clean work surface, roll out the clay with the rolling pin.

2. With a pencil draw the outline of the coin on the clay. Cut it out with the knife. Either air dry or bake the finished coins.

3. Paint the coins with the markers. First do one side, allow it to dry, and then paint the reverse side. Work on some newspaper so you can clean up easily.

4. With the black marker, copy the designs onto your coins.★

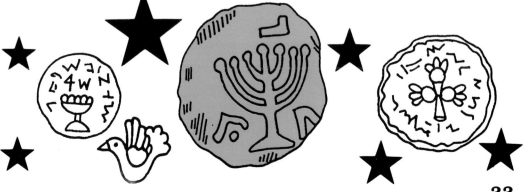

Star of David, Moon, Sun, Tree, and Dove Stencils

These easy-to-cut-out stencils can be used for decorating wrapping paper, T-shirts (if you use fabric paint and follow the directions to make the paint permanent), and Hanukkah cards. You could cut out a table runner from an old sheet or piece of muslin, and use gold fabric paint to make a Hanukkah table accessory. The stencil designs will pop out so quickly that you can cover a large area in a flash.

HERE'S WHAT YOU WILL NEED★

manila folder (to make the stencils)
pencil, tracing paper, scissors
paints or fabric paints, paintbrushes, sponges
masking tape, small dishes to hold paint
fabric or T-shirt, or assorted papers

HERE'S HOW TO DO IT★

1. To make the stencils, follow the directions on page 11. Trace the patterns that you want to use onto the manila folder. Leave about 2″ between designs on the folder.

2. With sharp scissors make a hole in the center of each design to begin cutting it out. Cut from the hole to the outside edges of the design. Do this for all of the designs.

3. Decide how you want to use the stencils and collect the materials you need. If you are decorating a T-shirt, place a piece of cardboard inside the shirt so that the fabric paints won't soak through to the back of the shirt. Tape the shirt down on your work surface. If you are making wrapping paper, also tape the paper down. To make a table runner, tape the fabric to a clean area on the floor. If you are making Hanukkah cards, fold your paper into the card shape first and then open it up.

4. Place your stencil on the material you want to decorate. You can tape down your stencil to make painting easier. Hold the stencil with one hand and dip the paintbrush into some paint. Lightly stroke the brush over the paper or fabric. Be sure to paint all the way to the edges. Hold the brush straight up so that less paint goes under the stencil.

5. Remove the stencil carefully. If you want to repeat the design, reposition it and paint it in again. Once the design is complete, allow the paint to dry. As you work you will discover how to space the designs and how you like to combine them. Experiment with different color paints also.★

Reuben's Tale, a Hanukkah Story from Long Ago

Hanukkah candles have been said to do miraculous things . . . and this is a story of how one person's life was saved by those little lights:

A long time ago, in a forest near a small Russian village, lived an old peddler named Reuben. Every day Reuben walked from village to village, carrying a large sack filled with copper and tin pots. He stopped at all the village homes, hoping to sell his wares.

One winter afternoon Reuben hurried home early. It was the last night of the Hanukkah festival and he wanted to begin the celebration with his family. But just as he started to sing the holiday songs and spin the dreidel with his children and grandchildren, he heard a knock at the cottage door.

Outside stood a messenger from the Count. Reuben was to come to the castle at once, bringing some of his fine copper pots.

Sadly, Reuben put on his heavy coat, picked up his sack, and said goodbye to his family. As he left, he tucked some Hanukkah candles into the sack. If he could not celebrate with his family, he would at least stop to light the candles on his trip home.

Reuben made his way through the forest to the castle. The Count had never seen such fine copper pots. He wanted them all, and gave Reuben a bag of silver coins in payment.

Happy with his success, Reuben started home. But it was very late, and very dark, and he was soon lost. He stumbled into a small clearing ringed by trees. There he settled in, to wait for morning to find his way home.

As he pulled his sack around himself to keep warm, he found the Hanukkah candles. Clearing the snow from the branch of a pine tree, he carefully placed nine candles on it. After singing the Hanukkah blessing, he lit the candles.

Suddenly, a strange feeling came over him. He began to feel afraid. He looked up and saw a line of large brown bears, moving in to circle the clearing.

At that moment the candle flames flared up. The snow-covered trees reflected the flames, as if they were mirrors. The bears stopped, frightened by the light, and turned and ran back into the forest.

All through the long winter night, the nine candles burned brightly, protecting the old peddler. When dawn came the forest seemed friendly again, and Reuben set off quickly for his cottage.★

A Picture Book of Reuben's Tale

We can make a decorated book with this Hanukkah folktale. It can be read and looked at after the family dinner, or given as a gift to a friend or relative.

HERE'S WHAT YOU WILL NEED★

3 sheets of white paper, 8½ × 11″
a pencil, black fine-line marker
tracing paper
crayons, watercolors, colored pencils
glue

HERE'S HOW TO DO IT★

1. Fold each sheet of paper in half along the 11″ side. Put a small amount of glue along the crease of one sheet and place the second sheet of paper on top of the first. Repeat this with the third sheet of paper.

2. Using the tracing paper, follow the directions on page 11 to trace the illustration of Reuben. Transfer the tracing to the cover of your book. Write the name of the folktale above it.

3. Open the book and start writing the folktale inside. Use all the pages for the story and put in pictures as you like.★

Chocolate Balls

These small candies can be enjoyed all through and after the Hanukkah celebration. You can also place some on a paper plate, wrap it in plastic, tie it with a bright ribbon, and presto! - you have a Hanukkah present for some lucky person.

INGREDIENTS★

2 tablespoons unsweetened cocoa powder
1 cup confectioners' sugar
2 tablespoons vanilla
2 tablespoons light corn syrup
2½ cups crushed vanilla wafers (Place 6 cookies on a piece of waxed paper, put another sheet of waxed paper on top, and gently crush with a rolling pin. Repeat with more cookies until you have 2½ cups.)
½ cup confectioners' sugar for coating the cookies

UTENSILS★

large mixing bowl
small mixing bowl
measuring cups and spoons
mixing spoons
rolling pin, waxed paper

HERE'S HOW TO DO IT★

1. Combine all the ingredients, except the last ½ cup of sugar, in the large mixing bowl. Stir until completely combined.

2. With clean hands, shape the mixture into balls about the size of large marbles. As you finish shaping them, place the balls on a sheet of waxed paper spread over your work surface.

3. Put the reserved ½ cup of sugar into a small bowl. Roll each ball in the sugar to coat it. Makes about 20 balls.★

Potato Latkes

Latke is the Yiddish word for pancake, and these crisp, golden-brown potato pancakes are a traditional treat during the Hanukkah celebration. They have a long history as the chief holiday delicacy. The oil they are fried in symbolizes the oil that miraculously burned for eight days in the Hanukkah legend. **This recipe requires help from an adult.**

HERE'S WHAT YOU WILL NEED★

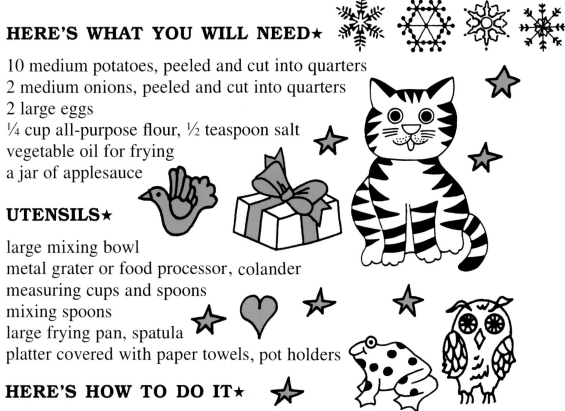

10 medium potatoes, peeled and cut into quarters
2 medium onions, peeled and cut into quarters
2 large eggs
¼ cup all-purpose flour, ½ teaspoon salt
vegetable oil for frying
a jar of applesauce

UTENSILS★

large mixing bowl
metal grater or food processor, colander
measuring cups and spoons
mixing spoons
large frying pan, spatula
platter covered with paper towels, pot holders

HERE'S HOW TO DO IT★

1. Soak the peeled, cut potatoes in a large bowl of water for a half hour or longer. Drain them well in the colander.

2. You can grate the potatoes and onions by hand using a metal grater (being very careful so you don't cut your fingers). Or, **with the help of an adult**, you can grate them in a food processor.

3. Put the grated potatoes and onions back into the large mixing bowl and add the eggs, flour, and salt. Mix well.

4. **Ask an adult to help you with the cooking.** Pour about 1″ of oil into the frying pan and heat it. As soon as it is hot, gently drop in a tablespoon of the potato mixture. You can probably fit in three more without crowding. When the pancakes are golden and crisp on the bottom, turn them over with the spatula. When the second side is crisp, remove them and place on a platter covered with paper towels, to drain off the cooking oil. Cook more batches as needed. Serve hot with applesauce. Serves 8–10 people.★

Note: You might find potato pancake mix in the supermarket. You won't need to grate the potatoes and onions. Follow the package instructions and fry as in step 4.

Hanukkah Cookies

These delicious Hanukkah cookies can be wrapped in pretty paper and given as a present. You can make patterns of the holiday symbols shown here to use for cut-out cookies. Or you can roll the dough with your hands into a 1″-wide log, cut off pieces, and shape them into Hebrew letters (see page 24). If you make letters, the baking time will be only about 7–10 minutes.

HERE'S WHAT YOU WILL NEED★

tracing paper, oaktag
pencil, scissors

INGREDIENTS★

1 cup sweet butter, softened
8-ounce package cream cheese, softened
¾ cup sugar
2 teaspoons vanilla
3½ cups flour
extra flour to roll out the dough
extra butter to grease the cookie sheets

UTENSILS★

large mixing bowl, mixing spoon
measuring cups and spoons
rolling pin, knife
cookie sheets
pot holders

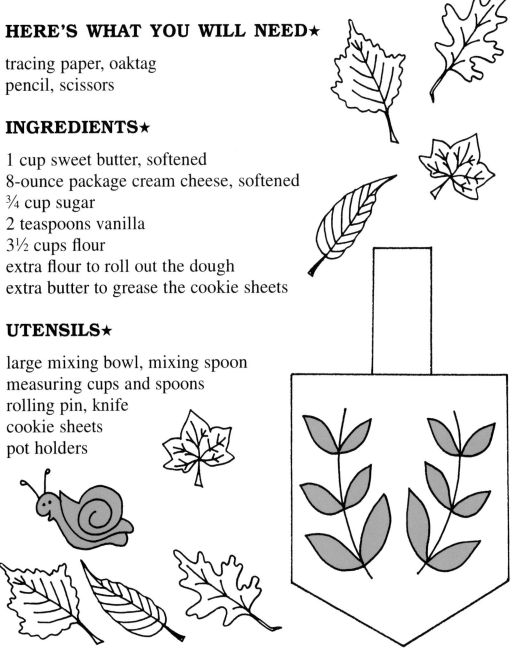

HERE'S HOW TO DO IT★

1.   Trace the patterns for the designs on tracing paper. Put the tracing paper on top of the oaktag and hold together with one hand. With the other hand, cut all around the outside edges. Cut out all of the designs until you have an oaktag pattern for each. Now start the cookies.

2.   **Preheat the oven to 350°F. Ask an adult to help you with this.** Stir the butter in the large mixing bowl until it is light and fluffy. Beat in the cream cheese, a little at a time.

3.   Add the sugar and vanilla. Add the flour and continue to stir until it is completely combined. You will have a nice stiff dough to work with.

4.   With the rolling pin, roll out the dough ¼″ thick on a lightly floured surface.

5.   Place a cardboard pattern on the rolled out dough. Hold it in place with one hand and cut all around the outside edge with a knife. Lift the pattern and repeat for the other designs. Make as many cookies of each design as you like.

6.   Place the cut-out cookies 1″ apart on greased cookie sheets. Bake for 10–15 minutes, or until lightly browned. Allow to cool. This makes about 24 cookies.★

Rugelach

Rugelach are half-moon shaped cookies with a melt-in-the mouth taste. If you put them on a pretty plate near the menorah, everyone can enjoy them after the candle lighting. A recipe very much like this was used in the 1600s.

INGREDIENTS★

½ cup sweet butter, softened
8 ounces cream cheese, softened
2 cups all-purpose flour
extra flour for rolling out the dough
extra butter to grease the cookie sheets

Raisin Nut Filling

½ cup sugar
½ cup raisins
1 teaspoon cinnamon
1 cup finely chopped nuts
¼ cup sugar (for topping)

Strawberry Jam Filling

1 cup strawberry jam
¼ cup sugar (for topping)

UTENSILS★

large and small mixing bowls
measuring cups and spoons
mixing spoon
plastic wrap
rolling pin, knife
cookie sheets
pot holders

HERE'S HOW TO DO IT★

1. In the large mixing bowl, combine the butter and cream cheese. Add the flour a little at a time and continue mixing until it is worked in.

2. Wrap the dough in plastic wrap and put it in the refrigerator for at least an hour.

3. **Preheat the oven to 350°F. Ask an adult to help you.** Choose the filling you want to use (raisin nut or strawberry jam). Prepare the filling by combining the ingredients (except the sugar for the topping) in the small bowl and set aside.

4. Take out the dough and cut into 2 parts. On a clean work surface spread the extra flour. With the rolling pin, roll out one half the dough until you have a circle, with the dough about ⅛″ thick. With a knife, cut the dough into 16 pie-shaped wedges, as shown. If the dough is too sticky, dust it with a little flour.

5. Sprinkle or spread the filling on each wedge. Beginning at the wide end, roll up the dough toward the point, as shown.

6. Grease the cookie sheets with butter. Place the cookies on the cookie sheets about 1″ apart. Sprinkle on some sugar for the topping.

7. Bake for 20–25 minutes, or until golden-brown. Makes 32 cookies.★

Index